Geronimo

THE INSPRING LIFE STORY OF AN
APACHE WARRIOR

BY BRENDA HAUGEN

COMPASS POINT BOOKS
a capstone imprint

Compass Point Books are published by Capstone,
1710 Roe Crest Drive, North Mankato, Minnesota 56003
www.mycapstone.com

Editorial Credits
Catherine Neitge and Angela Kaelberer, editors; Ashlee Suker, designer;
Wanda Winch, media researcher; Kathy McColley, production specialist

Photo Credits
Alabama Department of Archives and History, Montgomery, Alabama,
43, 87; Alamy: North Wind Picture Archives, 8; Bridgeman Images: ©
look and learn/Private Collection/Severino Baraldi, 7; Capstone, 10, 78;
Charles Deering McCormick Library of Special Collections, Northwestern
University Library, 94; Corbis, 74, Burstein Collection, 9, Tim Thompson,
101; Courtesy of artist Jeroen Vogtschmidt, 64; CriaImages.com: Jay Robert
Nash Collection, 81; The Denver Public Library: Western History Collection,
62; Getty Images: Bettmann, 4, 102, MPI, 50, 90, MPI/Camillus S. Fly,
55, The Life Picture Collection/US Signal Corps/Time Life Pictures, 41,
61; Granger, NYC – All rights reserved, 35, 44; Jeremy Rowe Vintage
Photography: Dudley Flanders Stereoviews, 59; Library of Congress: Prints
and Photographs Division, 12, 17, 23, 38, 52, 67, 68, 73, 75, 76, 84, 91, 97,
99, 103, 104, 105; National Archives and Records Administration (NARA),
92; Newscom: Picture History, 83; North Wind Picture Archives, 15, 24,
27, 29, 49, 71; Shutterstock: gudinny, design background, Philip Bird LRPS
CPAGB, 18; Western History Collections, University of Oklahoma Libraries,
Noah H. Rose Photograph Collection, [ROSE 885], 30

Library of Congress Cataloging-in-Publication Data
Names: Haugen, Brenda, author.
Title: Geronimo : the inspiring life story of an Apache warrior / by Brenda
Haugen.
Description: North Mankato, Minnesota : Compass Point Books, a Capstone
imprint, 2017. | Series: CPB grades 4-8. Inspiring stories | Includes
bibliographical references and index. | Audience: Ages 10-12. | Audience:
Grade 4 to 6.
Identifiers: LCCN 2016019213| ISBN 9780756551629 (library binding) |
ISBN 9780756551841 (ebook (pdf))
Subjects: LCSH: Geronimo, 1829-1909—Juvenile literature. | Apache
Indians—Kings and rulers—Biography—Juvenile literature. | Apache
Indians—Wars—Juvenile literature.
Classification: LCC E99.A6 H28 2017 | DDC 979.004/97250092 [B]—dc23
LC record available at https://lccn.loc.gov/2016019213

Table of Contents

Geronimo was known, and feared, throughout Mexico and the United States.

Chapter One

A BATTLE
IN MEXICO

It was a good day for a battle. Apache warriors and Mexican soldiers had skirmished the day before near the town of Arizpe in Sonora, Mexico. Neither side scored anything close to a victory, but late in the day, the Apaches captured the soldiers' supply train—a group of mules carrying loads of weapons, ammunition, and food. Armed with these extra supplies, the Apache were ready for battle the next morning.

Around 10 o'clock about 100 Mexican infantry and cavalry soldiers rode to meet about 200

Apache, who were positioned near a river. A young warrior in his late 20s led the Apache. His name was Goyahkla, which meant "one who yawns." All the Apache fought fiercely that day, but Goyahkla's strength and bravery were fueled by a burning desire for revenge. Mexican soldiers had killed his mother, wife, and three small children the year before, and he was convinced that the soldiers he was fighting that day were responsible.

After his family was killed, Goyahkla had a vision in which an unseen voice called him by name and said, "No gun can ever kill you. I will take the bullets from the guns of the Mexicans, so they will have nothing but powder. And I will guide your arrows." Goyahkla believed in the vision. He fought that day with no fear.

After two hours of fighting, Goyahkla and three other Apaches were left in a clearing with no guns, arrows, or spears—only their knives. Mexican soldiers closed in on them, quickly killing the other three warriors. As Goyahkla ran, he grabbed a spear and turned on a Mexican soldier, killing him. He then

Mexican soldiers killed Geronimo's family in 1851.

An Apache took aim at an approaching wagon.

grabbed the dead soldier's sword and brandished it
against another soldier. The two fell to the ground as
they fought, and Goyahkla killed the soldier with his
knife. He got up and waved the sword in the air as
he searched for more soldiers to attack. He fought so

fiercely that the Mexicans couldn't stop staring at him. They started yelling "Geronimo," the Spanish word for "Jerome." The reason has been lost over time, but some believe the Mexicans might have been shouting to Saint Jerome for help.

The Mexican soldiers soon retreated, after suffering 26 dead and 46 wounded. The great Apache victory in 1852 established Goyahkla as a fierce warrior. It also gave him the name he would use for the rest of his life—Geronimo.

SAINT JEROME

Born in northern Italy in about 340, Jerome was a doctor and priest. When barbarians attacked Rome in 410, Saint Jerome found safe shelter for many Roman Christians.

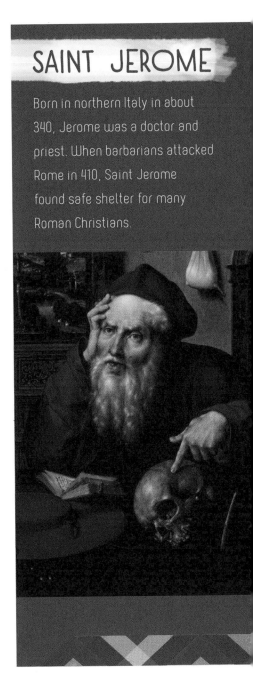

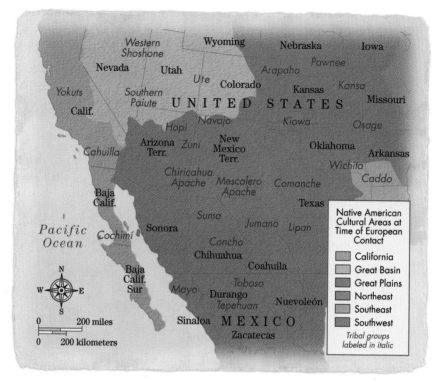

The Apache lived in Mexico and what would become the United States.

Geronimo became one of the most feared Apache warriors of all time. As Mexican and American settlers, explorers, prospectors, and troops moved onto Apache lands, Geronimo and other Apache fought to survive. The Apache raiders looted, burned, and murdered their way through Arizona and New Mexico as they crisscrossed the border between the United States and Mexico.

Newspapers added to Geronimo's legend with stories of savage attacks he and other Apache warriors carried out. Some of the stories were true, but many others proved false. In both the United States and Mexico, Geronimo was blamed for far more destruction and death than he ever caused. He became one of the most famous and feared American Indian warriors.

Cradleboards kept Apache babies safe and secure.

Chapter Two

AN APACHE
CHILDHOOD

Geronimo said he was born in June 1829 in the No-doyohn Canyon in present-day Arizona. Others say he was born in 1823. And since the Apache didn't keep track of days the way white people did, no one knows his exact date or year of birth. His father's name was Taklishim and his mother's name was Juana. They were members of the Bedonkohe band of the larger Chiricahua Apache tribe.

Taklishim, whose name meant "the gray one," was the son of Chief Mahko, who had been a great leader. Mahko had loved peace and was known for his generosity toward his people. Mahko died several years before Geronimo was born, but Taklishim told him many stories about his grandfather. Mahko was remembered as a brave warrior who fought against the Mexicans. But Taklishim said Mahko only fought the Mexicans after they attacked him first.

Geronimo and his family lived in a tepee made of antelope and deer hides. The animal hair on the hides helped keep the tepee waterproof. Their lives were relatively peaceful. White settlers hadn't yet come to their area. "During my minority we had never seen a missionary or a priest," Geronimo later said. "We had never seen a white man. Thus quietly lived the Be-don-ko-he Apaches."

Geronimo had one sister, Nah-dos-te, who was four years older than he was. He also grew up with many cousins, whom he considered his brothers and sisters. The children spent their days playing games outside. Their games involved skills that they would need to have as adults. They often pretended to be warriors

The Apache sometimes lived in dome-shaped dwellings known as wikiups.

fighting in battle. They also played hiding games. The Apaches' safety often depended on their ability to cover their tracks and hide in the mountain caves and crevices of their homeland. Geronimo said later:

> *"Frequently when the tribe was in camp a number of boys and girls, by agreement, would steal away and meet at a place several miles distant, where they could play all day free from tasks. They were never punished for these frolics; but if their hiding places were discovered they were ridiculed."*

Apache children didn't spend all their time playing, though. When they were about 5 or 6 years old, they started helping their parents with the daily chores that helped the tribe survive. The girls helped their mothers carry water and collect wood for fires. They also learned to cook and sew. Boys learned to care for the horses and make weapons and tools. They practiced shooting bows and arrows. The Apache both hunted animals and raised crops for food. Geronimo

THE LIFE GIVER

Geronimo learned as a child to pray to the Apache god, the Life Giver, also called Usen. The Apache believed that Usen would grant them strength, health, and wisdom. They also believed Usen protected the Apache people, but didn't get involved in their problems with other people. The Apache knew that they had to settle those themselves.

The Apache believed that Usen had taught their ancestors about herbs to use to treat illnesses. As they treated sick people, they prayed to Usen. Geronimo became skilled in using the herbs and treating warriors who were injured in battle. Some people considered him a medicine man.

Apache girls learned to make baskets from their mothers.

gathered nuts and berries with his mother and also

helped his father in the fields. He said:

> *"When we were old enough to be of real service, we went to*

Apache boys learned to hunt buffalo in their teens.

the field with our parents: not to play, but to toil. When the
crops were planted we broke the ground with wooden hoes.
We planted the corn in straight rows, the beans among
the corn, and the melons and pumpkins in irregular order
over the field.

"Melons were gathered as they were consumed. In the
autumn pumpkins and beans were gathered and placed in
bags or baskets; ears of corn were tied together by the husks,

and then the harvest was carried on the backs of ponies up to our homes. Here the corn was shelled, and the harvest stored away in caves or other secluded places to be used in the winter."

As soon as Geronimo proved he could handle a bow and arrow, he learned to hunt small animals, such as rabbits and wild turkeys. Most boys started hunting bigger game, such as deer and buffalo, with the men when they were about 14. But it's likely that Geronimo began hunting bigger game between the ages of 8 and 10 because of his skill in making and using weapons.

Normally Geronimo's father would train him to be a hunter and warrior. But when Geronimo was 10, Taklishim died after a long illness. No one knows who stepped in to help Geronimo complete

AN APACHE FUNERAL

Geronimo's father was buried in a cave with his possessions according to Apache burial custom. The Apache believed a person's belongings went with him or her into the next world. The cave's entrance was then sealed with rocks.

the rest of his training. It may have been one of his father's half-brothers or another man of the tribe.

After his father's death, Geronimo was responsible for providing for his mother, even though he was just a boy. His sister, Nah-dos-te, had married and gone to live with her husband's family. "My mother chose to live with me, and she never desired to marry again," he said later. "We lived near our old home, and I supported her."

Geronimo wanted more than anything to be a warrior. When a young Apache man felt he was ready, he volunteered to go with the older warriors into battle. He had to successfully participate in four battles with the help of an experienced warrior who acted as a mentor. Instead of actively fighting in the battles, the young men watched and learned from their mentors and the other warriors. Geronimo completed his fourth battle when he was 17. He became part of the council of warriors, meaning he could fully participate in battles.

Geronimo also was considered old enough to get married. He visited his cousin Ishton, who lived with the Nednai band of Apache in the Sierra Madre of Mexico. Ishton was married to a Nednai man named Juh, who was one of Geronimo's best friends. While Geronimo was with the Nednai, he fell in love with a beautiful Nednai girl named Alope.

Geronimo asked Alope's father, No-po-so, for permission to marry her. No-po-so told Geronimo he could marry Alope in exchange for a gift of many ponies. "I made no reply,

AN IMPORTANT LESSON

Life in the desert was full of danger, and people had to be careful. Geronimo learned this lesson as a boy gathering berries with his mother and other women. One day a woman wandered away from the group. No one noticed she was missing until her pony showed up back at the camp. The pony was loaded with baskets but missing its rider.

Several Apache went out looking for the woman and eventually found her. A bear had attacked her. As her dog snapped at the growling creature, the woman stabbed the bear several times, and it ran away. She was badly injured, but the camp's medicine man used healing herbs to nurse her back to health.

but in a few days appeared before his [home] with the herd of ponies and took with me Alope," Geronimo recalled. "This was all the marriage ceremony necessary in our tribe."

The newlyweds went to live with Geronimo's people. He built a new tepee near the one where his mother lived. Alope decorated the inside of the tepee with beads and paintings. Within a few years, the young couple had three children. Geronimo was happy, but that happiness wouldn't last.

Life at a Glance

DATE OF BIRTH: June 1829

BIRTHPLACE: No-doyohn Canyon, Arizona

FATHER: Taklishim

MOTHER: Juana

EDUCATION: No formal education

SPOUSES: Alope, Ta-ayz-slath,
Nana-tha-thtith, Chee-hash-kish,
She-gha, Shtsha-she, Zi-yeh,
Ih-tedda, Azui

CHILDREN: Three killed at a young age
Chappo
Dohn-say (Lulu)
Lenna
Robert
Eva
Fenton

DATE OF DEATH: February 17, 1909

PLACE OF BURIAL: Apache Cemetery,
Fort Sill, Oklahoma

U.S. forces defeated Mexican soldiers in battle, which led to the end of the Mexican War in 1848.

Chapter Three

TRAGEDY

AND REVENGE

Geronimo and his people lived in an area that various groups of people had been fighting over for years. Texas declared its independence from Mexico in 1835 and formed its own national government the next year. Mexico didn't recognize the Republic of Texas. Mexican leaders also wanted to keep the United States from annexing Texas as a territory or state.

Many people in the United States, however, believed in Manifest Destiny—the idea that their country would one day stretch all the way across North America, from the Atlantic to the Pacific oceans. Mexican land stood between the United States and this destiny. The United States annexed Texas, which became a state in 1845. This led to the Mexican War.

The Apache paid little attention to the war between the two countries. They didn't believe it would affect them. But the Treaty of Guadalupe Hidalgo, which ended the war in 1848, forever changed the lives of the Apache.

Under the treaty, the United States agreed to pay Mexico $15 million for the more than 525,000 square miles (1.3 million square kilometers) of land that was at issue. The lands included California, Utah, Nevada, parts of Colorado and Wyoming, and most of Arizona and New Mexico—places that Geronimo and his fellow Apache called home. And as part of the treaty, the United States promised to keep the American Indians from attacking Mexican settlements and towns. But that wasn't an easy promise to keep.

The Apache lived by hunting animals, especially buffalo, and growing crops. But when they were

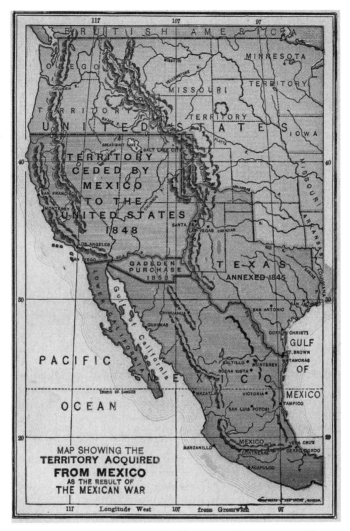

After the war the United States gained land from Mexico that would become all or part of seven states.

low on supplies or needed horses, they would stage raids on enemy tribes. When Spanish settlers came to Mexico, the Apache raided them as well. Geronimo probably obtained the ponies that he gave Alope's father through a raid on a Mexican ranch or village.

Some Apache, including the Nednai, remained in Mexican territory. Government officials in the Mexican state of Chihuahua believed that if the Nednai had what they needed, they would stop making raids. The officials invited the Nednai to trade in their communities and even set up a system for passing out rations and supplies.

The plan seemed to work. The Nednai traded animal hides and furs for cloth and tools. But sometimes they traded stolen goods. Colonel José Maria Carrasco, the new military commander in the Mexican state of Sonora, believed that the Nednai were raiding Sonoran towns and trading the goods in Chihuahuan towns. He was determined to stop them.

Other Apache heard of the trade agreement between the Chihuahuans and the Nednai. Mangas Coloradas, the leader of the Warm Springs band of Apache, decided to go to Mexico to trade. Geronimo and several others joined him. Because the trip was

Portraits of an Apache chief (from left), medicine man, and war chief

meant to be a peaceful trading mission, the men
brought their families with them.

The group headed for the Mexican city of Casas
Grandes, with a stop in the town of Janos. The
Mexican government was scheduled to distribute
supplies and gifts to the Apache in Janos, and Mangas
and his people wanted to be there when the goods
were handed out.

Mangas, son of Apache leader Mangas Coloradas

Mangas Coloradas' group camped outside of Janos. Each day the men traveled into Janos for supplies, returning to camp at night. The women and children stayed behind at the camp, guarded by a few warriors.

Late on the afternoon of March 5, 1851, the Apache men returned to their camp as usual. They were met by a few of their women and children, who had a terrible tale to tell them. Carrasco and his soldiers had attacked the camp, killing the guards first. They then raided the camp, stole supplies and horses, killed more than 20 people, and took at least 60 others prisoner. Most of these people were women and children.

Geronimo and the rest of the men hid until nightfall, when they crept back into the camp. He discovered his mother, wife, and three children among the dead. Geronimo's heart was broken. He would never be the same person again.

"I had no weapon, nor did I hardly wish to fight, neither did I contemplate recovering the bodies of my loved ones, for that was forbidden," Geronimo said later.

The remaining Apache returned to their home along the Gila River. Geronimo was overwhelmed with anger and sadness.

"Within a few days we arrived at our own settlement," he said. "There were the decorations that Alope had made—and there were the playthings of our little ones. I burned them all, even our tepee. I also burned my mother's tepee and destroyed all her property. I was never again contented in our quiet home. I had vowed vengeance upon the Mexican troopers who had wronged me, and whenever I … saw anything to remind me of former happy days my heart would ache for revenge upon Mexico."

After he burned all of his family's belongings, Geronimo went off alone and cried. As he sat alone, he said he heard a voice calling his name. Geronimo couldn't see anyone, but the voice told him that he would be protected in battle and that his arrows would be guided to kill the Mexican soldiers. This vision gave

MEXICAN COMMANDER

Colonel José Maria Carrasco led the raid on the Apache camp where Geronimo's family was killed. He was appointed commander and inspector of the military colonies in Sonora in 1851.

Carrasco viewed all Apache as uncivilized murderers and thieves. He believed Geronimo and his friends had been conducting raids in Sonora. As commander of Sonora's military, Carrasco took about 400 of his men into the nearby state of Chihuahua to capture the Apache he believed had committed crimes in his state.

The people in Chihuahua lived in peace with the Apache camped near Janos. Leaders of the two groups had signed a treaty June 24, 1850. Chihuahuan officials believed the Apache people had lived up to their side of the bargain. They doubted Carrasco's story that the Apache had murdered and robbed people. In fact, the Sonorans were probably right. It's likely that Geronimo and the other Apache had been involved in the raids in Sonora.

The Apache usually raided only if they were out of supplies and desperate for food. So government officials in Chihuahua spent a great deal of money on rations and other supplies to keep the Apache from raiding their cities. The Chihuahuan officials didn't want the Sonorans to ruin the peace and stir up trouble. But Carrasco brushed aside their opinions. Believing there was no such thing as a peaceful Apache, he ordered his men on March 5, 1851, to attack the Apache camp where Geronimo lived.

him courage and increased his desire to avenge his
family members' deaths.

Mangas Coloradas called a war council to decide
what the Apache should do. Because he had lost the
most family members, the council members picked
Geronimo to meet with leaders of the other Apache
tribes. He asked them to join the war party. Many of
them agreed after hearing Geronimo's story. They
included Cochise, the great chief of the Chiricahua,
as well as Geronimo's friend Juh, who was now the
Nednai chief.

The warriors decided to attack the city of Arizpe in
Sonora. As about 200 warriors set up camp outside of
the town, people in the city became frightened. Eight
men volunteered to go out to the Apache camp and
see what they wanted. But the Apache warriors had
no intention of talking over things peacefully. They
were there for revenge. As the town representatives
came close to the camp, the Apache killed them. The
Apache knew that killing the townspeople would lure
the Mexican soldiers into attacking their camp.

Cochise, leader of the Chiricahua Apache

Geronimo asked to act as war chief for the battle, even though he was still young and inexperienced. The chiefs agreed and named Geronimo war chief out of respect for his suffering. "I was no chief and never had been, but because I had been more deeply wronged than others, this honor was conferred upon me, and I resolved to prove worthy of the trust," Geronimo later said.

The next day about 100 Mexican troops marched out to attack the camp. The battle lasted for two days. On the second day, the Mexican commander called in the cavalry to help his soldiers. Geronimo and the other Apache became even angrier when they saw the cavalry members ride in. They believed these cavalrymen were the ones who had slaughtered their families in Janos.

After a fierce battle, Geronimo and the other Apache scored a victory. He had revenge for the deaths of his family—but it wasn't enough. His anger toward the Mexican government and people would last the rest of his lifetime and push him into some poor decisions.

CHEATING DEATH

After the battle at Arizpe, Geronimo still hated the Mexicans and yearned for revenge. He decided to conduct another raid several months after the battle. He asked two other warriors, Ah-koch-ne and Ko-deh-ne, to help him carry it out.

The three warriors sneaked into a Sonoran village early in the morning. Seeing five horses hitched to a post, they decided to steal them. As they crept toward the horses, they believed no one had spotted them. Just then, shots rang out from nearby buildings. Ah-koch-ne and Ko-deh-ne died in the hail of bullets. Geronimo had to run for his life.

The Mexicans chased Geronimo on horseback and on foot, but his keen hiding skills kept him safe. Having used all his arrows, he carried only a knife for protection. He feared falling asleep and being discovered, so he forced himself to stay awake.

By the time he arrived home, Geronimo was exhausted and hungry. When he showed up without Ah-koch-ne and Ko-deh-ne, some of his people were angry. They blamed him for the deaths of the two warriors. He said later that the failed raid made other warriors hesitate to join him on future attacks.

Geronimo was almost killed during another Mexican raid. After slipping in a pool of blood, Geronimo felt the butt of a gun slam into his head. He fell to the ground, unconscious. When the battle ended, other Apache warriors found Geronimo and helped him to his feet. Despite his injuries, Geronimo made it back to camp without help, but he carried the scar for the rest of his life. "In this fight we had lost so heavily that there really was no glory in our victory, and we returned to Arizona," Geronimo remembered. "No one seemed to want to go on the warpath again that year."

Artist Frederick Remington's depiction of Geronimo and his band returning from a raid in Mexico

Chapter Four

THE WHITE

INVASION

Until the Mexican War, Mexicans were the only outsiders that Geronimo and his people had to deal with. After the war ended, though, the U.S. government sent surveyors to explore the huge tract of land the country had received under the Treaty of Guadalupe Hidalgo. The surveyors were the first white people Geronimo had ever seen. He said:

> "We gave them buckskin, blankets, and ponies in exchange
> for shirts and provisions. We also brought them game,
> for which they gave us some money. We did not know the
> value of this money, but we kept it and later learned from

the Navajo Indians that is was very valuable. Every day they measured land with curious instruments and put down marks which we could not understand. They were good men, and we were sorry when they had gone on into the west. They were not soldiers. These were the first white men I ever saw."

Geronimo's first experience with white Americans was a good one. But that wouldn't always be the case. In 1848, gold had been discovered in California, which at the time was home to about 150,000 American Indians, 6,500 Latinos, and fewer than 1,000 whites. By the beginning of 1850, 100,000 settlers and immigrants seeking

APACHE GOLD

Gold was a magic word to many Europeans and Mexicans. They would lie, cheat, steal, and even kill to get their hands on the precious metal that was worth so much money. The Apache couldn't understand the thinking. Gold was too soft to make bullets or arrowheads, so it was little use to them. Also, they considered gold sacred to their god, Usen. Apache beliefs allowed them to pick up loose gold from the ground, but not to dig into the earth to find it.

Cavalry soldiers were stationed at Fort Bowie, which was built near Apache Pass in 1862.

gold and fortune had poured into California. Some of them traveled through the Dragoon and Chiricahua mountains of southeastern Arizona using the Apache Pass—which was located in the land belonging to Chief Cochise's people, the Chiricahua Apache.

Cochise kept the path open, but never promised anyone safe passage. But people kept traveling through the pass. It was located near a freshwater spring, which was vital for people on the long journey to California.

At the time, Geronimo was living among Cochise's people. He had married a woman named Chee-hash-kish. A well-known and respected chief, Cochise stood 6 feet 2 inches (188 centimeters) tall, a giant among the Apache people. Like most men of the time, Geronimo was about 5 feet 9 inches (175 cm).

During his time with the Chiricahua, Geronimo participated in a number of raids on Sonoran ranches and towns. He also took another wife, Nana-tha-thtith. Apache men could marry as many women as they were able to support. Having more than one wife was a sign of wealth.

As time went on, Geronimo decided to move his family farther north and join Mangas Coloradas and the Warm Springs band in what is now New Mexico. Geronimo's family included the children he had with Chee-hash-kish—a son, Chappo, and

Chappo, the son of Geronimo

a daughter, Dohn-say. He also had one more child
with Nana-tha-thtith. But moving north didn't take
them away from trouble with whites. Unlike the
whites heading through Apache Pass on their way

The Apache fought with white settlers taking over their land.

to California, the people who settled near the Warm Springs band had no intention of leaving. They were there to mine the rich deposits of silver, copper, and other minerals. Because the miners hoped the ore would make them rich, they cared little for the rights of the American Indians who lived on the land.

The Apache responded by killing travelers in the area. Still, the miners wouldn't leave.

Gold was discovered in Bear Creek in 1860 and miners quickly built the town of Pinos Altos in New Mexico Territory. The U.S. Army founded Fort McLane nearby to help keep peace between the miners and American Indians. Meanwhile, the U.S. government was planning to move southwestern tribes, including the Apache, onto smaller reservations. The move would leave the remaining land open to white development and settlement.

Mangas Coloradas hoped to keep the peace between the white settlers living on his people's land. But that didn't happen. In December 1860 a group of about 30 miners attacked a Bedonkohe encampment near the Mimbres River. The miners, who believed the Apache had stolen their livestock, killed four people and wounded and captured several others. The actions set off a series of attacks between the miners and the Apache. The chiefs and their warriors killed travelers,

FELIX WARD

Felix Ward's kidnapping played a major role in the fates of Cochise and Mangas Coloradas. Felix was born around 1850, the son of a Mexican woman whom the Apache had taken captive. His biological father was unknown. Because he was said to have red hair, some people believed his father was a white man. Others said his father was an Apache. Whatever the case, Felix and his mother escaped the Apache and ended up living with white rancher John Ward about 40 miles (64 km) southeast of Tucson, Arizona.

Historians aren't sure if Felix was kidnapped from the ranch or if he ran away from home and was picked up by the Apache. He lived with the Apache until he was grown. When he was in his mid-20s, he changed his name to Mickey Free and became an interpreter and a scout for the U.S. Army. He spoke English, Spanish, and Apache well enough to communicate between the three groups, but none of them really trusted him. He served as interpreter in at least one of Geronimo's meetings with army officials. Ward died alone and penniless in 1915 in Arizona at about age 65.

burned wagons, and captured livestock. The miners fought back by attacking the Apache camps.

Geronimo participated in raids against whites, but his focus remained making the Mexicans pay for the suffering they had caused him. But in February 1861, something happened that also hardened him against whites. At that point, Geronimo was back living with the Chiricahua in Apache Pass.

A group of Apache warriors allegedly stole livestock and kidnapped an 11-year-old boy named Felix Ward from a ranch in the Sonoita Valley in January 1861. Felix was the stepson of the ranch's owner, John Ward, and was believed to be of mixed Mexican and Apache heritage. Ward told U.S. soldiers at Fort Buchanan that Cochise and his men had kidnapped his stepson.

Army Second Lieutenant George Bascom and about 50 soldiers traveled to Apache Pass to confront Cochise. On February 4 Cochise agreed to talk to Bascom at the army camp. Believing the meeting would be a friendly one, Cochise brought his family with him—his wife and two children, as well as his brother Coyuntura and two nephews. Bascom accused Cochise and his warriors of carrying out the raid and kidnapping the boy. Cochise denied being involved, but said that if Bascom gave him a week, he could likely persuade the Apache who had kidnapped Felix to return him to his father. Bascom told Cochise that he and his people would remain hostages until the boy and the livestock were returned.

To avoid being taken prisoner for something he didn't do, Cochise quickly cut a hole in Bascom's tent with his knife and escaped. Surprised by Cochise's sudden move, the soldiers couldn't catch him. One of Cochise's nephews tried to escape as well, but the soldiers were ready this time. They clubbed him and stabbed him with a bayonet. The others were trapped.

The next day Geronimo and Mangas Coloradas joined Cochise. They took four whites—a stagecoach employee and three teamsters—as hostages after killing six Mexican teamsters. Cochise told Bascom he'd exchange the four men for his relatives. When Bascom refused to negotiate, Cochise killed his

An Apache collected rattlesnake venom to use to poison arrows. The arrows were used in hunting and warfare.

prisoners. Bascom responded by hanging Cochise's brother and nephews, although his wife and children were eventually released.

Tragedy also struck the Warm Springs band in January 1863. Geronimo and his family were living with them again, under Mangas Coloradas' leadership. Mangas was ready to talk peace despite Geronimo's warning not to trust the whites. As a compromise, Mangas agreed to take half the band with him to talk

Geronimo (right) and members of his band

peace at Fort McLane. The remaining Apache would
stay at the camp under Geronimo's leadership and
await word from Mangas.

Pretending they wanted a truce, a group of soldiers
and some miners from Pinos Altos lured Mangas from
the rest of the group. They captured the chief and
then tortured and killed him. Soldiers killed the other

Apache who had traveled with Mangas. Geronimo awaited news from Mangas. If the whites were telling the truth, Geronimo would lead the rest of the band to join Mangas and the others. Geronimo said:

"No word ever came to us from them. From other sources, however, we heard that they had been treacherously captured and slain. In this dilemma we did not know just exactly what to do, but fearing that the troops who had captured them would attack us, we retreated into the mountains near Apache Pass."

After Mangas' death, Geronimo gained power. Mangas had trusted the whites and paid with his life. Geronimo's distrust of the soldiers proved to be valid. Tribe elders started asking Geronimo's opinions. While the United States now proved itself the enemy of the Apache, Geronimo's hatred of Mexicans still burned deep within him. He wanted revenge for all the people he had lost.

The U.S. effort to settle the Southwest was put on hold while its soldiers fought the Civil War.

Chapter Five

MOVING TO THE RESERVATION

For four years, the American Indians in the Southwest didn't have to worry too much about clashes with the U.S. Army. After Abraham Lincoln was elected president of the United States in 1860, 11 southern states left the United States and formed their own government, the Confederate States of America. From 1861 to 1865, the Union and the Confederacy fought the bloody Civil War. The army needed every available man to fight the battles. But when the war ended, the government could again turn its attention to settling the Southwest and dealing with American Indian issues.

To free land for white settlers, the U.S. government decided to send native people to reservations. The government expected the Indian people to live, hunt, and raise crops on the land, instead of moving from place to place as they had been accustomed to for hundreds of years.

Geronimo's old friend Cochise came to a peace agreement with the U.S. Army in 1872 and agreed to move his people to a reservation. The army established the Chiricahua Apache Reservation about 15 miles (24 km) south of Fort Bowie in Arizona Territory. Cochise liked and trusted the army's agent, Captain Tom Jeffords. Cochise convinced Juh and Geronimo to bring their people to live on the reservation as well. Cochise had promised Jeffords that the Apache on the reservation wouldn't conduct any raids within Arizona Territory. In return, Jeffords distributed supplies to the Apache on a regular basis and also allowed them to leave and return to the reservation when they wanted.

Juh and Geronimo kept Cochise's promise to leave Arizona ranches and towns alone. But they still regularly raided Sonora in Mexico. Their actions upset Jeffords, who told Cochise that if the raids didn't stop, his people could lose their reservation. Cochise told Geronimo, Juh, and the rest of the warriors in late 1873 that they either needed to stop raiding Mexico or leave. Geronimo and Juh decided to leave. They took their people and moved into Mexico.

Geronimo and members of his band were fierce fighters.

Cochise died in June 1874, probably of stomach cancer. His son Taza took over, but he wasn't able to unite the band the way his father had. Soon warriors were again conducting raids in Mexico.

The government wanted to set aside one reservation for all American Indians living in Arizona and southwest New Mexico. Leaders said creating just one reservation would cut down on government costs. But the idea to establish just one reservation was probably more about keeping more land for white settlements and mining than about saving the government money.

The government had established the San Carlos Reservation in southwestern Arizona in 1872. Having one reservation for several tribes was a problem in itself. Some of the tribes were enemies who fought against each other. But that didn't matter to the government. Government leaders expected the tribes to settle their differences and live in peace on the reservation.

More than 4,000 American Indians from various tribes were living at San Carlos by 1876. In June

FRIEND OF THE APACHE

Thomas Jeffords was born in New York in 1832. He went west in 1858 to work on the railroads. By 1862 he was working as an army scout in New Mexico and Arizona. In 1867 he set up a meeting with Cochise at Cochise's camp. Jeffords had learned some of the Apache language and treated Cochise with respect at the meeting, turning over his weapons to assure Cochise that he had come in peace. The two men talked for two or three days and became friends. The Apache called Jeffords Tyazalaton, which meant "red beard" or "sandy whiskers."

Army General Oliver Howard wanted to negotiate a peaceful transfer of Cochise and his people to a reservation in 1870. He asked Jeffords to help him because of his friendship with the Apache leader. Cochise agreed to move to the reservation only if Jeffords would act as the army's agent for the reservation. Jeffords was reluctant to take the job, but agreed in order to stop the fighting between whites and the Apache.

He spent four years as Indian agent at the reservation, and Cochise and his people repaid his kind treatment by living in peace with the soldiers and settlers in Arizona. Jeffords visited Cochise the day before he died in June 1874, and Cochise asked Jeffords to take care of his people after his death. Jeffords did his best, but in 1876 the army replaced him as agent with John Clum. Cochise's band had to move to the San Carlos Reservation, but their move was peaceful, largely because of their respect for Jeffords.

After leaving the army, Jeffords worked as a stagecoach driver, deputy sheriff, and gold miner in Arizona. He died in 1914 and is buried in Tucson.

Geronimo and his people were told that they had to go to the reservation. Instead of moving, Geronimo again led his band into the mountains of Mexico. He continued raiding Mexican towns. As a result, in early 1877, Commissioner of Indian Affairs John Smith ordered Geronimo and his followers arrested for robbery and murder and brought to San Carlos to be jailed.

Sergeant John Clum was the agent in charge of San Carlos. In April 1877 he was working on moving the Apache living at the Ojo Caliente Reservation in New Mexico Territory to San Carlos. On April 21 Clum invited Geronimo to a meeting at Ojo Caliente. By tricking Geronimo into believing he only wanted to talk, Clum became the only person ever to capture Geronimo. "The messengers did not say what they wanted with us, and as they seemed friendly we thought they wanted a council and rode in to meet the officers," Geronimo later said.

Geronimo and his followers brought their wives and children to meet Clum and his men. There to greet

John Clum (center) and Apache scouts at the San Carlos Reservation

him were Clum and about 20 policemen from the White Mountain Apache. At the meeting, Clum told Geronimo he intended to jail him and his warriors, not only for their refusal to stay at San Carlos, but for killing men and stealing livestock.

Geronimo replied, "We are not going to San Carlos with you, and unless you are very careful, you and your Apache police will not go back to San Carlos either. Your bodies will stay here at Ojo Caliente to make food for coyotes."

After Geronimo finished speaking, Clum signaled 80 soldiers and Apache policemen to come out of their hiding places. Geronimo and his people were trapped. Clum grabbed Geronimo's rifle while others took the guns from the remaining native leaders. The rest of the group peacefully laid their weapons on the ground.

Clum and his men forced the group to travel to San Carlos. The trip took about three weeks. Geronimo and 18 other Apache leaders were shackled and thrown into the jail at San Carlos on May 20, 1877. Clum ordered the rest of Geronimo's people to set up camp on the reservation. Life at San Carlos was miserable for the Apache. They were exposed to deadly diseases, such as smallpox and malaria, which claimed many lives.

Geronimo and the other men remained in prison for three months. During that time Clum was

Soldiers stood guard as Apache men dug a ditch at the San Carlos Reservation.

determined that the prisoners would be hanged for
their crimes, and did all he could to make that happen.
Clum held Geronimo responsible for the deaths of
more than 100 people and felt the leader's death
would save the lives of countless others.

But Clum's wish didn't come true. Feeling
unappreciated by the U.S. government, he quit his job
on July 1, 1877. A few weeks later, Indian inspector

Life was not easy for the Apache at the San Carlos Reservation.

William Vandever, who was running the reservation after Clum left, released Geronimo and the other prisoners. They were still required to stay at San Carlos, though. But in September the warrior Victorio and his followers escaped San Carlos. They eventually ended up back at Ojo Caliente.

Geronimo remained at San Carlos. He felt loyalty not only to his people, but also to those whom Cochise had led. While Geronimo was in jail, Cochise's son Taza had died. His younger brother Naiche was his replacement as chief. But Naiche had even less leadership experience than Taza. Geronimo befriended Naiche and gave him advice on how to lead his people.

Henry Hart arrived in August as the new Indian agent at San Carlos. Hart wanted to help the Indians and the army repair their relationship. Geronimo, Naiche, and the other leaders promised Hart that they would stay on the reservation.

Disease continued to plague the Apache, as did lack of food and decent clothing. To escape their misery, the men made a homemade alcohol drink from corn called tiswin. Geronimo and a group of men were drunk on tiswin August 1, 1878, when Geronimo and one of his nephews began arguing. The nephew, upset that he had offended his uncle, committed suicide. Upset and ashamed, Geronimo gathered his wives and children and escaped the reservation. Joining with his friend Juh, Geronimo led his people into the Sierra Madres.

Geronimo (center) and his followers were the last Apache holdouts.

chapter six

GERONIMO
THE HUNTED

By the time Geronimo fled into the Sierra Madres, his family had grown. Sometime after 1865 he had married a relative of Cochise, She-gha. He also took another wife, named Shtsha-she. In the mid-1870s Mexican soldiers took his wife Chee-hash-kish prisoner during a raid. He then married a Nednai woman named Zi-yeh. The wives added more children to his family.

Geronimo's wives and children usually stayed in the mountains when he went out on raids. He would raid for supplies, but also show up at the reservations when his raids were unsuccessful or when rations were being distributed. To some he was a hero, a man who lived according to his own rules. To others, he was a savage killer. Geronimo also had enemies among his own people. Many Apache blamed him for the difficulties and deaths that the tribe had suffered. They said when Geronimo arrived he stirred up trouble and encouraged other men to join him. Samuel Kenoi, the son of one of Geronimo's men, said later:

"Pretty soon he would raid a settlement here, or kill a person, and the whole tribe would be blamed for it. Instead of coming and getting his rations and settling down and trying to be civilized, he would be out there like a wild animal, killing and raiding. Then they would organize the Chiricahua scouts and send them out after Geronimo's men. In this way he caused Apache to fight Apache and all sorts of trouble to break out among our people."

Eventually, the U.S. government grew tired of Geronimo's raids. Army General George Crook

General George Crook served in the Civil War before being sent west.

was given the job of traveling to Mexico to capture
Geronimo and his followers in 1883.

Crook left for Mexico on May 1 with a crew of 42
soldiers, 193 Apache scouts, nine officers, 266 mules,
and 76 men in charge of the animals and supplies.
They traveled through a wasteland. "For three days we
did not see a human being," Crook said. "The whole

Geronimo and Naiche posed on horseback in 1886. Perico, one of Geronimo's best fighters, held a baby. Tisnah stood at right.

country had been laid waste by the Apaches and much land of value and formerly cultivated had grown into a jungle of cane and mesquite."

The Mexican people living in the areas Crook traveled through were tired of living in fear of Geronimo and his raids. They told Crook and his crew that they hoped he would capture Geronimo and the other Apache living in the area.

Crook reached the area of the mountains where Geronimo was living in mid-May. A number of people at the Apache camp came to the army camp to surrender. Geronimo came to the camp May 20, and asked to speak to Crook, who refused to talk to him until the next day.

When the two men finally met, Geronimo told Crook he wanted peace but the terrible conditions at the San Carlos reservation forced him to leave. He admitted to attacking Mexican communities but shared the reasons that he hated the Mexican people. Crook listened but didn't let Geronimo off easily. He angrily reproached Geronimo about the problems he and his men had caused. He also held Geronimo responsible for conducting raids in the United States and killing American settlers. Geronimo insisted that he had killed only Mexicans. But he didn't seem to have much fight in him. He finally told Crook, "We give up, do with us as you please."

Geronimo agreed to return to the United States and try reservation life again. But it took him a while to get there. The Chiricahua chiefs wanted to wait until all of their people had returned to their camp before making the trip to San Carlos. They continued to raid Mexican communities for the horses and supplies that they needed. Geronimo's old friend Juh and his people joined the camp in June, uniting the Chiricahua bands in one place. But 35 Chiricahuas were still being held captive in the Mexican town of Chihuahua City. Geronimo tried to persuade the Mexicans to return the captives, but he was unsuccessful. The Chiricahuas left their camp in October. Sadly, Juh wasn't with them. He had been killed in September when he and his horse ran off a trail and fell into the Casa Grandes River.

Geronimo and his people didn't reach San Carlos until February 1884. Geronimo and the other men tried to farm. The reservation land wasn't very good farmland, but Geronimo did his best for a while, raising a variety of produce.

Food was distributed at the San Carlos Reservation, where living conditions were poor.

Geronimo never completely trusted the agents and army officers running the reservation, though. It took only a rumor of trouble for him to fear that he might again be put in prison, and he would take off for Mexico. During one of his escape attempts, soldiers captured Geronimo's wives and several of his children. Geronimo then stole a Mescalero Apache woman named Ih-tedda from her tribe and married her.

In late 1885 the U.S. government again sent Crook to bring in Geronimo. Crook met with Geronimo in March 1886 in Sonora and gave him a choice. He could either surrender or die fighting. "You must make up your own mind whether you will stay out on the warpath or surrender unconditionally," Crook said. "If you stay out, I'll keep after you and kill the last one, if it takes fifty years." Under the deal Crook offered the Apache, they wouldn't be allowed to return to San Carlos right away. Instead, they would be transported to a reservation in Florida for two years. After that, they could return to Arizona.

Geronimo formally surrendered March 27, saying, "Once I moved like the wind. Now I surrender to you and that is all." The next day Crook returned to the United States. He left Lieutenant Marion Maus in charge, with instructions to bring the Apache to Fort Bowie in southeastern Arizona. But that wasn't going to happen. The night before, a bootlegger named Charles Tribolett provided whiskey to the Apache. A smuggler as well as a bootlegger, Tribolett traded

Geronimo (seated, third from left) met with Crook and his men to negotiate a surrender.

with the Apache raiders. He didn't want to lose their business. He likely convinced Geronimo and several others that they were better off running away than going to Fort Bowie and then to Florida. Geronimo and Naiche gathered their families and a few other people and left the camp on foot for the Sierra

Madres. They walked in small groups on rocks so that they wouldn't leave a trail for the soldiers to follow.

Maus ordered an officer and some scouts to take the remaining Apache to Fort Bowie. At Fort Bowie, when Crook learned that Geronimo had again escaped,

The Apache were held prisoner at Fort Bowie.

General Nelson A. Miles replaced Crook in the quest to capture Geronimo.

he asked for a transfer to a different post. Brigadier General Nelson A. Miles replaced him April 11. Miles was determined to do what no one else had ever done—bring in Geronimo and keep him from ever leaving again.

HARPER'S WEEKLY.

JOURNAL OF CIVILIZATION.

Vol. XXX.—No. 1616.
Copyright, 1886, by Harper & Brothers.

NEW YORK, SATURDAY, JANUARY 9, 1886.

TEN CENTS A COPY.
$4.00 PER YEAR, IN ADVANCE.

The hunt for Geronimo was featured on the cover of Harper's Weekly *in 1886.*

chapter seven

FINAL

SURRENDER

General Miles came prepared. He had 5,000 soldiers—about one-fourth of the entire U.S. Army—on hand to capture Geronimo and his band of 17 Apache. As Geronimo and Naiche moved into Mexico, they continued their raids.

Miles sent Lieutenant Charles Gatewood after Geronimo in July 1886. With the help of Chiricahua scouts, Gatewood followed Geronimo's trail in Mexico. Gatewood had two problems. He had to find Geronimo without being killed, and he also had to get around Mexican officials who didn't want Americans searching for Geronimo. The Mexicans wanted to be the ones to kill him.

A scout reported to Gatewood on August 23 that he'd found Geronimo's people in the Torres Mountains about four miles (6.4 km) away. Gatewood went to Geronimo's camp the next morning. Geronimo said he'd surrender if he and his people were allowed to go back to the reservation and not be punished. He also asked that they receive

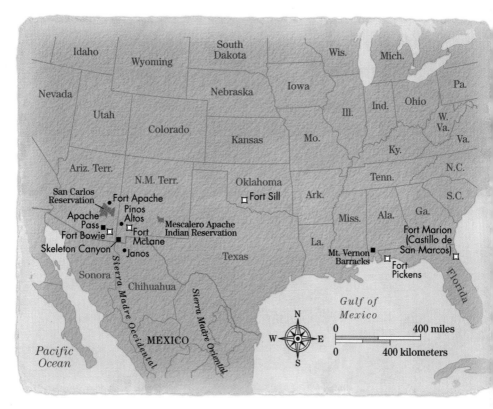

Geronimo and his followers would be sent across the country after their capture.

food, clothing, and farm tools. Gatewood thought Geronimo's terms seemed fair, but he couldn't agree to them. General Miles hadn't given him the right to negotiate with the Indians. "If I was authorized to accede to these modest propositions, the war might be considered at an end right there," Gatewood later said.

All Gatewood could offer Geronimo was to be transferred to Fort Bowie and have a chance to reunite with family members who had been captured earlier. Gatewood warned Geronimo that if he didn't accept Miles' terms, fighting would likely continue. Geronimo replied that he wouldn't surrender until he talked personally with General Miles.

Miles met with Geronimo on September 3, 1886, at Skeleton Canyon near the Arizona-New Mexico border. Miles promised Geronimo that his past crimes would be pardoned and that he and his people would be sent to Florida, where they would remain together.

Geronimo asked for a night to think it over. The next morning, he agreed to Miles' terms. "I will quit the warpath and live at peace hereafter," he said. The men left September 5 for Fort Bowie. Geronimo told Miles that this trip was the fourth time he surrendered. "And I think it is the last time," Miles replied.

Geronimo, Naiche, and 25 other Apache boarded a train September 8 to travel to Florida. But two days later, the train stopped in San Antonio, Texas. Soldiers led the Apache to a fenced-in area with tents. It would be their home for the next 42 days.

Crowds of curious people gathered around the fenced area for a glimpse of the Apache. They were especially eager to see Geronimo, whom they had read about in the papers. After a time the soldiers allowed small groups of people inside to look at the Apache.

During their time in San Antonio, Geronimo and the other warriors asked over and over again when they would be allowed to join their families in Florida, as Miles had promised them. The soldiers told them that they were waiting on word from President Grover Cleveland, whom the Apache knew as the Great White Father in Washington. Geronimo was especially

Geronimo (front, third from right) and Naiche (front, third from left) and their followers were shipped by train to a Florida prison.

concerned about his wife Ih-tedda, who was pregnant with their first child.

While the men waited, their families had gone on to Florida without them. The whole experience was overwhelming for the native people. Many had never seen a train before, let alone traveled across the country in one. Nearly 400 Apache were packed into

10 train cars. The hot, smelly cars became a breeding ground for disease. Many people became infected with tuberculosis on the long train ride.

Finally, on October 22, President Cleveland made his decision. Geronimo and the others who were considered criminals would be sent to Fort Pickens on an island in Pensacola Bay, Florida. The rest of the group stayed in Fort Marion, 300 miles (483 km) away in St. Augustine, Florida. Miles' promise of a reservation where they could all live together was broken.

According to Secretary of War William Endicott, Cleveland felt honoring Miles' agreement with Geronimo would be too risky:

"By direction of the President it is ordered that the hostile Apache adult Indians ... be sent under proper guard to Fort Pickens, Florida, there to be kept in close custody until further orders. These Indians have been guilty of the worst crimes known to the law ... and the public safety requires that they should be removed far from the scene of their [crimes] and guarded with the strictest vigilance.

Geronimo (from left), Naiche, and Mangas in captivity at Fort Pickens in 1887

The remainder of the band captured at the same time, consisting of eleven women, six children, and two enlisted scouts, you are to send to Fort Marion, Florida, and place with other Apache Indians recently conveyed to and now under custody at that post."

Geronimo was still in San Antonio when Ih-tedda gave birth to their daughter Lenna at Fort Marion. It would be a long time before he learned of her birth or heard any news of his family.

Geronimo was one of the most photographed American Indians of his day.

Chapter Eight

LIVING

IN EXILE

Life was difficult for the families at Fort Marion. Coming from the dry desert, they weren't used to the humid Florida climate. They didn't have enough food and became sick with tuberculosis, malaria, and other diseases.

In 1887 the War Department told the Apache at Fort Marion who had family at Fort Pickens that they could join them there. Geronimo finally reunited with his wives and children April 27. But that September, Geronimo's wife She-gha died from tuberculosis. She likely caught the disease while living at Fort Marion.

The Apache at Fort Marion who didn't have relatives at Fort Pickens were moved to Mount Vernon Barracks in Alabama. When the Apache arrived in Alabama, Major William Sinclair saw that many of them were sick and starving. They had been forced to sell the few things they owned just to buy food. Sinclair protested the Apaches' treatment to his supervisors. The army finally sent full military rations for the starving Apache. They also allowed the Indians to build small log cabins instead of making them live in tents.

In May 1888 Geronimo and the other Apache at Fort Pickens were sent to Mount Vernon Barracks as well. Finally, the Chiricahua were all together in one place, as General Miles had promised them almost two years earlier.

Later that year Geronimo faced a difficult decision. The Mescalero Apache asked that their people who were included in the roundup of Geronimo and his people be allowed to return to New Mexico. The War Department agreed. Geronimo's wife Ih-tedda was

Apache prisoners at Mount Vernon Barracks in 1890

a Mescalero. Allowing her and their daughter Lenna
to go to New Mexico meant that they would be free.
Ih-tedda was pregnant, which made Geronimo's
decision even more difficult. He knew he might never
see Ih-tedda or Lenna again or meet the new baby.
But he knew that returning to New Mexico would be
the best thing for all of them.

"So many of our people died that I consented to let one of my wives go to the Mescalero Agency in New Mexico to live," he said. "This separation is according to our custom equivalent to what the white people call divorce, and so she married soon after she got to Mescalero. She also kept our two small children, which she had a right to."

Geronimo's unselfish decision may have saved his children's lives. Lenna and Robert, nicknamed Robbie, were the only two of Geronimo's many children who lived long enough to raise families of their own.

Geronimo and the remaining Apache were sent to Fort Sill, Oklahoma, on October 4, 1894. Geronimo was excited by the prospect of moving to a place where he could have a patch of land to farm. He said:

"I want to go somewhere where we can get a farm, cattle, and cool water. I have done my best to help the authorities— to keep peace & good order to keep my house clean. ... Young men old men women and children all want to get away from here—it is too hot and wet—too many of us die here. ... Every one of us have got children at school and

INDIAN SCHOOLS

At Fort Marion, many children were forced to leave their parents and attend school. Some went to a Catholic school in the city. Student James Kaywaykla remembered, "[The] Catholic Sisters undertook to teach the children a little English, and provided baths, clothing, and sometimes medicine," he said. "I will never forget the kindness of those good women, nor the respect in which we held them. For the first time in my life I saw the interior of a church and dimly sensed that the White Eyes, too, worshipped Usen."

Nearly 100 Indian youth were sent much farther away to the Carlisle Indian School in Pennsylvania. At least one-fourth of the young people became sick with tuberculosis and died. Among them was Geronimo's oldest surviving son, Chappo, who died in 1894 at age 30.

In February 1889 the army opened a school at Mount Vernon staffed by two young teachers. The children no longer had to be torn from their parents to go to a school where many of them felt like outcasts.

Some of Geronimo's other children attended the school. He understood the importance of getting an education in the world in which they now lived. He made sure the children behaved and listened to their teachers. He also encouraged the boys to play such American sports as football and baseball.

Geronimo and his family farmed small plots of land at Fort Sill, Oklahoma.

we will behave ourselves on account of these children, we want them to learn. I do not consider that I am an Indian any more. I am a white man and [would] like to go around and see different places. I consider that all white men are my brothers and all white women are my sisters—that is what I want to say."

TELLING HIS STORY

Geronimo became friends in 1904 with S. M. Barrett, the school superintendent in Lawton, Oklahoma. Through interpreter Asa Daklugie, son of Chief Juh, Geronimo shared with Barrett many memories of his life. Barrett then asked if he could publish the memories as a book. Because Geronimo was technically still a prisoner, he had to get permission from the army officer in charge of him, who refused. Barrett then wrote to President Theodore Roosevelt, who gave his permission

with the condition that the book would be reviewed by the War Department before it was allowed to be published. Geronimo's autobiography, titled *Geronimo's Story of His Life*, was published in 1906.

Geronimo dedicated the book to President Roosevelt:"Because he has given me permission to tell my story; because he has read that story and knows I try to speak the truth; because I believe that he is fair-minded and will cause my people to receive justice in the future; and because he is chief of a great people, I dedicate this story of my life to Theodore Roosevelt."

After his 1886 capture Geronimo remained a prisoner the rest of his life.

While the Apache had small plots of land on which to raise crops and cattle, many of them were still becoming sick and dying. Geronimo believed his people would never regain their health until they were allowed to return to the Southwest. "We are vanishing from the earth," he said. "The Apaches and their homes each [were] created for the other by Usen himself. When they are taken away from these homes they sicken and die. How long will it be until it is said, there are no Apaches?" Despite his pleas, Geronimo and the other Apache at Fort Sill remained captive.

Geronimo posed for famed photographer Edward S. Curtis in 1905.

chapter nine

THE FINAL
YEARS

Throughout his life, Geronimo had dealt with loss. After he was captured, he spent the rest of his life trying to get back to the Southwest. "I want to go back to my old home before I die," Geronimo told a newspaper reporter in 1908. "Tired of fight and want to rest. Want to go back to the mountains again. I asked the Great White Father to allow me to go back, but he said no."

Geronimo's family was very important to him. He grieved quietly for the wives and children he had lost to violence and disease, including his daughter Dohn-say, who had taken the American name Lulu. She died in 1898 at Fort Sill, leaving a young son, Thomas. Geronimo took care of Thomas, and the two became close. When his wife Zi-yeh died of tuberculosis in 1904, Geronimo also took over the care of his 5-year-old daughter, Eva, and the household. Geronimo experienced a major blow when Thomas died March 11, 1908, at age 18. Geronimo didn't show much emotion, but he was never the same after Thomas' death.

As the Apache discovered when they were first captured and sent to Fort Bowie, many white Americans were curious about them. Geronimo decided to use the interest to earn money. Although still a guarded prisoner, Geronimo traveled the country, appearing at fairs and exhibitions. He showed his skill at making bows and sold what he made, along with photos and autographs. People were even interested in his coat buttons as souvenirs. He'd pluck off the buttons but always kept a supply with him to sew back on and sell to others.

Geronimo was skilled at making bows and arrows, a craft he practiced all his life.

In 1898 Geronimo appeared as an attraction at
the Trans-Mississippi and International Exhibition in
Omaha, Nebraska. He was invited to appear at the
St. Louis World's Fair in 1904. He later recalled:

> *"When I was at first asked to attend the St. Louis World's
> Fair I did not wish to go. Later, when I was told that I*

would receive good attention and protection, and that the President of the United States said that it would be all right, I consented. I sold my photographs for twenty-five cents, and was allowed to keep ten cents of this for myself. I also wrote my name for ten, fifteen, or twenty-five cents, as the case might be, and kept all of that money. I often made as much as two dollars a day, and when I returned I had plenty of money—more than I had ever owned before."

Geronimo headed to Washington, D.C., in 1905. President Theodore Roosevelt had asked Geronimo to participate in his second inaugural parade. Geronimo thought his participation in the parade was a great honor. But Roosevelt was apparently just using him for publicity. A newspaper reporter sat next to Roosevelt as he watched the parade in front of the White House. "To him I said, 'Why did you select Geronimo to march in your own parade, Mr. President? He is the greatest single-handed murderer in American history,'" the reporter recalled. "To which he characteristically replied, 'I wanted to give the people a good show.'"

Geronimo (second from right) rode in Theodore Roosevelt's inaugural parade.

By the winter of 1908–1909, Geronimo was showing his age. His short, muscular frame began to shrink, and he started to forget things. He also wasn't as active as he had been in the past. But he kept on making bows and arrows, his fingers as nimble as ever.

Geronimo headed into Lawton, Oklahoma, on February 11, 1909, to sell some of his bows and arrows. He used some of the money he earned to buy whiskey. After drinking, he decided to ride home in the

CONGRESS HONORS GERONIMO

In February 2009, 100 years after Geronimo's death, the U.S. House of Representatives passed a resolution that honored the life of Geronimo, "his extraordinary bravery, and his commitment to the defense of his homeland, his people, and Apache ways of life." House Resolution 132 also acknowledged the many wrongdoings of the United States against Geronimo and the Apache people. Geronimo's life ensured that the struggles of the Apache will never be forgotten.

dark. Along the way he fell off his horse and landed partly in a creek. He lay there until morning, when a person passed by and found him.

After the cold, wet night, Geronimo developed pneumonia. Doctors doubted he would live long. He asked that his children Eva and Robert be allowed to come to Fort Sill from their boarding school near Ponca City, Oklahoma. He wanted to see them before he died. Geronimo clung to life as he waited for them, but the army doctor had sent them the news in a letter instead of a telegram. They didn't reach Fort Sill until the day of his funeral.

Geronimo is buried in the Apache Cemetery at Fort Sill, Oklahoma.

Geronimo died early the morning of February 17, with Apache friends at his bedside. He was 79. He was buried in the Apache Cemetery at Fort Sill, next to Zi-yeh and other members of his family. A rock monument marks Geronimo's grave. A large eagle made of rock is at the top of the monument. A symbol of the freedom Geronimo treasured, it's a fitting marker for the final resting place of the famous warrior.

Timeline

1829
Born in June in present-day Arizona

1851
His mother, wife, and three children are killed by Mexican troops in a March 5 massacre

1863
Mangas Coloradas, who fought with Geronimo, is murdered

1846
Becomes a warrior after he turns 17 and marries his first wife, Alope

1878

Geronimo is among a group of Apache that flee San Carlos and run to the mountains of Mexico

1877

Geronimo and his family are captured; Geronimo is jailed at San Carlos

1876

Flees with his family to Mexico to avoid going to the San Carlos Reservation

1886

Surrenders to General Nelson Miles at Skeleton Canyon and is eventually sent to Florida

Timeline

1898

Geronimo is an attraction at the Trans-Mississippi and International Exhibition in Omaha, Nebraska, the first of many similar events

1887

Sent to Mount Vernon Barracks in Alabama

1894

Arrives with his people at Fort Sill in Oklahoma

1906
Autobiography is
published

1909
Dies February 17 at Fort Sill

1905
Rides in President Theodore
Roosevelt's second-term
inaugural parade

Glossary

annex—claim authority over the land of another nation

cavalry—soldiers who travel and fight on horseback

hostage—person taken by force and held, often as a way to obtain something

interpreter—person who hears one language and translates its meaning to another

malaria—a serious disease that people get from mosquito bites; malaria causes high fever, chills, and sometimes death

mentor—wise and faithful adviser or teacher

raid—sudden, surprise attack on a place

reservation—area of land set aside by the U.S. government for American Indians; in Canada reservations are called reserves

revenge—action taken in return for an injury or offense

surveyor—someone who measures areas of land for builders or mapmakers

tuberculosis—disease that affects the lungs and causes fever, cough, and difficulty breathing

warrior—person trained to fight in battles

OTHER BOOKS IN THIS SERIES

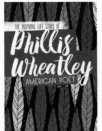

Further Reading

Bodden, Valerie. *Apache.*
Mankato, Minn.: Creative Education, 2015.

Niver, Heather Moore. *The Life of Geronimo.*
New York: PowerKids Press, 2016.

Sanford, William R. *Apache Chief Geronimo.*
Berkeley Heights, N.J.: Enslow Publishers, Inc., 2013.

Spilsbury, Richard. *Geronimo.* Chicago: Raintree, 2014.

Internet Sites

Use FactHound to find Internet sites related to this book. All of the sites on FactHound have been researched by our staff.

Here's all you do:

Visit www.facthound.com

Type in this code: 9780756551629

Source Notes

Page 6, line 12: David Roberts. *Once They Moved Like the Wind: Cochise, Geronimo, and the Apache Wars*. New York: Simon and Schuster, 1993, p. 111.

Page 14, line 12: Angie Debo. *Geronimo: The Man, His Time, His Place*. Norman: University of Oklahoma Press, 1976, p. 18.

Page 15, line 5: S. M. Barrett, ed. *Geronimo's Story of His Life*. New York: Duffield & Company, 1906, p. 25.

Page 17, line 3: Alexander B. Adams. *Geronimo*. New York: Putnam, 1971, p. 49.

Page 20, line 6: *Geronimo's Story of His Life*, pp. 36-37.

Page 21, line 21: *Geronimo: The Man, His Time, His Place*, p. 31.

Page 31, line 19, C. L. Sonnichsen, ed. *Geronimo and the End of the Apache Wars*. Lincoln: University of Nebraska Press, 1990, p. 36.

Page 32, line 6: *Geronimo: The Man, His Time, His Place*, p. 37.

Page 35, line 4: *Geronimo's Story of His Life*, p. 52.

Page 37, line 25: *Geronimo: The Man, His Time, His Place*, p. 49.

Page 39, line 9: Ibid., p. 46.

Page 51, line 5: *Geronimo's Story of His Life*, p. 121.

Page 58, line 16: *Geronimo: The Man, His Time, His Place*, p. 105.

Page 59, line 6: Ibid., p. 105.

Page 66, line 11: *Geronimo and the End of the Apache Wars*, p. 72.

Page 67, line 6: *Geronimo: The Man, His Time, His Place*, p. 178.

Page 69, line 20: Robert Utley. *Geronimo*. New Haven: Yale University Press, 2012, p. 140.

Page 72, line 4: *Geronimo: The Man, His Time, His Place*, p. 259.

Page 72, line 14: *Geronimo*, p. 185.

Page 79, line 4: *Geronimo and the End of the Apache Wars*, p. 62.

Page 79, line 20: *Geronimo*, p. 306.

Page 80, line 3: Ibid., p. 293.

Page 82, line 15: Ibid., p. 308.

Page 88, line 1: Ibid., p. 342.

Page 88, line 16: Ibid., pp. 360-361.

Page 89, line 3: *Geronimo*, p. 319.

Page 91, line 20: *Geronimo's Story of His Life*, dedication page.

Page 93, line 5: Ibid., p. 378.

Page 95, line 3: *Geronimo*, p. 313.

Page 97, line 5: *Geronimo's Story of His Life*, p. 197.

Page 98, line 16: *Geronimo and the End of the Apache Wars*, p. 119.

Page 100, line 5: House Resolution 132. 111th Congress (2009-2010). 23 Feb. 2009. https://www.congress.gov/bill/111th-congress/house-resolution/132/text

Select Bibliography

Adams, Alexander B. *Geronimo*. New York: G.P. Putnam's Sons, 1971.

Barrett, S. M., ed. *Geronimo's Story of His Life*. New York: Duffield & Company, 1906.

Debo, Angie. *Geronimo: The Man, His Time, His Place.* Norman: University of Oklahoma Press, 1976.

Hirsch, Mark. "Too Long a Way Home: Healing Journey of the Chiricahua Apaches." *American Indian*. Summer 2008. http://blog.nmai.si.edu/main/2011/05/too-long-a-way-home-healing-journey-of-the-chiricahua-apaches.html

Jackson, Ron. "Stories of the Ages: Geronimo." *The Oklahoman*. NewsOK. http://ndepth.newsok.com/geronimo

"Old Apache Chief Geronimo is Dead." *The New York Times*. 18 Feb. 1909, p. 7. http://www.nytimes.com/learning/general/onthisday/bday/0616.html

Roberts, David. *Once They Moved Like the Wind: Cochise, Geronimo, and the Apache Wars*. New York: Simon and Schuster, 1993.

Santee, Ross. *Apache Land*. Lincoln: University of Nebraska Press, 1971.

Sonnichsen, C. L., ed. *Geronimo and the End of the Apache Wars*. Lincoln: University of Nebraska Press, 1990.

Utley, Robert M. *Geronimo*. New Haven: Yale University Press, 2012.

Index

~ Index cont.

~ CRITICAL THINKING USING THE COMMON CORE ~

1. The Apache and the other American Indian groups had their way of life
   disrupted when European settlers arrived. How would you feel if something
   like this happened to you? How would you react? (Integration of Knowledge
   and Ideas)

2. The U.S. government broke many promises to the Apache and other
   American Indian groups. How did these broken promises affect the decisions
   Geronimo and other American Indians made? (Integration of Knowledge
   and Ideas)

3. Some people admired Geronimo for the many things he did to help his
   people. Others said he was a murderer and thief who caused trouble
   wherever he went. What kind of person do you think he was? Support your
   answer with evidence from the text. (Key Ideas and Details)